Phonics Focus: long e (ie)

THE MOVIE

BY CHRISTINA EARLEY

ILLUSTRATED BY
ANASTASIA KLECKNER

A Blue Marlin Book

SEAHORSE PUBLISHING

Introduction:

Phonics is the relationship between letters and sounds. It is the foundation for reading words, or decoding. A phonogram is a letter or group of letters that represents a sound. Students who practice phonics and sight words become fluent word readers. Having word fluency allows students to build their comprehension skills and become skilled and confident readers.

Activities:

BEFORE READING

Use your finger to underline the key phonogram in each word in the *Words to Read* list on page 3. Then, read the word. For longer words, look for ways to break the word into smaller parts (double letters, word I know, ending, etc.).

DURING READING

Use sticky notes to annotate for understanding. Write questions, make connections, summarize each page after it is read, or draw an emoji that describes how you felt about different parts.

AFTER READING

Share and discuss your sticky notes with an adult or peer who also read the story.

Key Word/Phonogram: movie

Words to Read:

niece	meanie
brief	Minnie
achieved	movie
brownies	moxie
collie	outfield
cookies	pieces
cowrie	relieved
eerie	retrieves
foodie	rookie
genie	smoothies
goalie	softie
Gracie	zombie
hankie	calories
hoodie	cockatiel
infield	kielbasa
Katie	

"Let's watch a movie," Katie says to her niece.

"Yes!" Gracie responds. "I will make the smoothies. You bake the cookies."

"Oh, Minnie, you are such a softie," Gracie says as she cuddles with Minnie the border collie on the couch.

Katie covers herself in her hoodie blanket. "What movie should we see first?" she asks.

"What is that zombie movie about?" asks Katie.

"It is about zombies playing baseball," Gracie explains. "Look at this brief clip. A player in the outfield retrieves the ball. Then, he throws it to the infield to stop the home run."

"I don't want to be a meanie, but that sounds eerie," Katie says. "How about that movie with a genie?"

"I know the one," says Gracie. "A rookie goalie finds a special cowrie in a hankie. A genie comes out of the shell and grants wishes to the goalie."

"Oooh! Let's watch this movie about a cockatiel," Katie says. "He is a foodie with moxie. To save calories, he tastes only small pieces. He loves kielbasa and brownies."

"We have achieved agreement," says Gracie. "I am relieved!"

Quiz:

1. **True or false?** The movie Katie and Gracie decide to watch is about a baseball game.
2. **True or false?** Katie is Gracie's aunt.
3. **True or false?** The dog is named Moxie.
4. What is the genre of this book? How do you know?
5. Why do Katie and Gracie decide not to watch the zombie movie? What clues in the story tell you?

Flip the book around for answers!

Answers:

1. False
2. True
3. False
4. **Possible answer:** It is realistic fiction because it is a pretend story about things that people do in real life, such as watching movies at home.
5. **Possible answer:** Katie does not like scary movies. She says that the zombie movie sounds eerie.

Activities:

1. Write a story about the movie that sounds most interesting to you.

2. Write a new story using some or all of the "ie" words from this book.

3. Create a vocabulary word map for a word that was new to you. Write the word in the middle of a paper. Surround it with a definition, illustration, sentence, and other words related to the vocabulary word.

4. Make a song to help others learn the long e sound of "ie."

5. Design a game to practice reading and spelling words with "ie."

Written by: Christina Earley
Illustrated by: Anastasia Kleckner
Design by: Rhea Magaro-Wallace
Editor: Kim Thompson
Educational Consultant: Marie Lemke, M.Ed.
Series Development: James Earley

Library of Congress PCN Data
The Movie (ie) / Christina Earley
Blue Marlin Readers
ISBN 979-8-8873-5001-1 (hard cover)
ISBN 979-8-8873-5060-8 (paperback)
ISBN 979-8-8873-5119-3 (EPUB)
ISBN 979-8-8873-5178-0 (eBook)
Library of Congress Control Number: 2022944994

Printed in the United States of America.

Seahorse Publishing Company
seahorsepub.com

Copyright © 2024 **SEAHORSE PUBLISHING COMPANY**

All rights reserved. No part of this publication may be reproduced, stored in a retrieval system or be transmitted in any form or by any means, electronic, mechanical, photocopying, recording, or otherwise, without the prior written permission of Seahorse Publishing Company.

Published in the United States
Seahorse Publishing
PO Box 771325
Coral Springs, FL 33077